Bradwell's ECLECTICA

A FEAST OF FUN, FACTS AND HISTORY!

SOUTHAMPTON

AF234514

Published by Bradwell Books
9 Orgreave Close Sheffield S13 9NP
Email: books@bradwellbooks.co.uk

Bradwell's Eclectica is a registered trade mark
of NMD Trading, Sheffield. UK.
® Number. UK 00003048225

British Library Cataloguing in Publication Data: a
catalogue record for this book is available from the
British Library.

1st Edition

ISBN: 9781909914582

Design by: Andrew Caffrey

Print: Gutenberg Press, Malta

Photograph Credits: Shutterstock, iStock, Creative
Commons and credited individually. All other
images are © the author.

Cover Image: Gary Davies Maritime Photographic

www.maritimephotographic.co.uk

Mapping: Ordnance Survey Mapping used under
licence from the Ordnance Survey.

Ordnance Survey Partner Number 100039353

Acknowledgements

Thanks to my niece, Jessica Garner, who, as a recent
graduate of Southampton University, and still
resident in the city, has been an invaluable on-tap
resource, willingly sharing her ideas and experiences.
Thanks also to my partner, Tony, for his enthusiasm,
his camera, and his willingness to enthuse about
the history of the 'Saints'! My family in general
are extraordinarily patient with my extended and
unsociable 'absences' from family life… perhaps
they're trying to tell me something!

Thanks, too, to Chris Gilbert of Bradwell Books
for his stoic patience; the next one will be on time,
Chris, promise!

Bradwell's ECLECTICA

A FEAST OF FUN, FACTS AND HISTORY!

SOUTHAMPTON

Linda Fernley

Contents

SHUTTERSTOCK/APRIL909

SHUTTERSTOCK

ISTOCK

WALKS

Visit the monuments in the town's tranquil Centre Parks or follow the ancient city walls to get a flavour of this historic city.

LOCAL EVENTS

Find out about some of the things that make Southampton special, and that bring visitors back year after year.

LOCAL HISTORY

So much to say and so little space … a smattering of Southampton's history will hopefully whet your appetite to dig a bit deeper!

GHOST STORIES

If you like to be spooked out, then these ghost stories will do the trick. If spectral soldiers and grey ladies aren't your cup of tea, skip this section!

LOCAL SPORTS

Southampton is home to the successful 'Saints' football club, and where Hampshire Cricket Club play their home games; and of course, you can find any type of water sport along the city's coast.

FAMOUS LOCALS

Comedian, politician, artist, actor, film director … and the man who took football to Brazil! Read all about Southampton's locals.

INTRODUCTION

WELCOME TO SOUTHAMPTON ... OR 'SOTON'!

Over the years, the city's name has been abbreviated in writing to **'So'ton'** or **'Soton'**, and so its residents are often referred to as **'Sotonians'**. Soton, the 'cruise capital of Europe', has over four million visitors a year; when you visit, you'll understand why. It has a rich heritage as an important UK port, and today handles a large proportion of the UK's national container freight, as well as world-famous cruisers, including the **Queen Mary** and the less fortunate **Titanic**.

Queen Mary iStock

West Quays

It also has lots to offer those in search of culture, from museums, music venues and art galleries to award-winning parks and the general hustle and bustle of a diverse city with top-class shopping facilities.

Southampton is home to the longest surviving stretch of medieval walls in England, as well as a number of outstanding museums such as **Tudor House Museum, Southampton Maritime Museum, the Medieval Merchant's House** and **Solent Sky**.

The **SeaCity Museum** focuses on Southampton's trading history and on the **RMS Titanic,** which embarked on its doomed maiden voyage from Southampton, carrying over 750 Sotonians, more than three-quarters of whom perished when the ship hit an iceberg off the coast of Newfoundland. The town pays homage to the disaster through a series of memorials (see the 'Walk' section further on in this book).

Mayflower Theatre

Southampton's links with the sea.

The city's 2,300-capacity **Mayflower Theatre** is the largest outside London and has hosted West End shows such as *Les Misérables, The Rocky Horror Show* and *Chitty Chitty Bang Bang*, as well as frequent appearances from the **National Opera** and **National Ballet companies**.

The city boasts two universities and a range of impressive art galleries: **Southampton City Art Gallery** at the Civic Centre houses a nationally important collection, while the Millais Gallery can be found at Southampton Solent University, and the John Hansard Gallery at Southampton University.

The **Southampton Boat Show** is held in September each year, attracting thousands of visitors and exhibitors to the **Mayflower Park** on the city's waterfront. The Boat Show itself is the climax of Sea City, which runs from April to September to celebrate

In August 2009, work began on a huge project to create a Cultural Quarter in the city's centre, on land adjacent to the

Guildhall; this is due to be completed in 2015 and looks set to compete favourably with any of the UK's other major cultural centres.

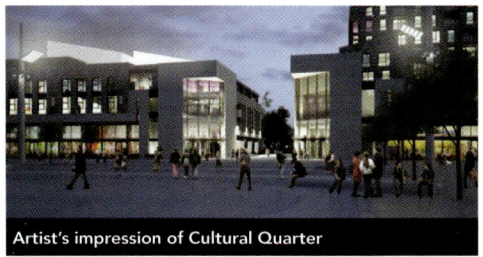

Artist's impression of Cultural Quarter

As well as boasting the country's largest oil refinery at Fawley, the city is also the greenest in Southern England! Southampton Common has over 300 acres of flora and fauna, and has hosted a huge array of shows, festivals, concerts, *BBC Springwatch, Race For Life, Sport Relief*, circuses, the *Ideal Home Exhibition*, drive-in movies and regular holiday fairs and markets. In the city centre there are five interconnected parks. One of them, **Watts Park**, has a statue to its namesake, the famous hymn writer **Isaac Watts**, and his

hymn *'O God, our Help in Ages Past'* echoes across the park from the Civic Centre clock tower three times a day! **East Park** has a large memorial to the engineer officers of the **Titanic**, none of whom survived.

Over the years, the town has become a magnet for shoppers – **West Quays** is a huge complex with an array of retail outlets, while **Ocean Village** is amongst the largest and most impressive in the whole of the country, located close to the **Red Funnel Ferry Terminal**. Lovers of seafood will drool at the marina's many restaurants, while coffee shops with impressive views, plenty of boats and yachts to be admired or hired, two large cinemas and the restored **SS Shieldhall** steamship keep visitors entertained.

A book of this size can do no more than touch on some of the things that make Southampton the exciting and vibrant city that it is today, and scrape

Ocean Village Marina iSTOCK

the surface of what makes its people 'tick'. However, I hope that as you dip in and out of the book, your appetite will be whetted to find out more for yourself. Come along to cheer on the Saints at a football match, watch some world-class cricket or attend one of the city's waterside events or activities.

Take part in the popular guided walks of the Old Town, discover the city's rich history at the **SeaCity Museum** or **Tudor House and Garden**, and explore the city on the self guided trails - the Titanic Walk or the QE2 Mile.

Whatever you do, I'm fairly sure you'll want to come back!

LOCAL DIALECT

THERE'S A GENERAL BELIEF THAT HAMPSHIRE IS A 'POSH' COUNTY, WHOSE INHABITANTS SPEAK IN A 'QUEEN'S ENGLISH' ACCENT.

While there appears to be no such thing as a specific Southampton accent or dialect, the Hampshire 'burr' is often recognised in natives of the town. There's a general belief that Hampshire is a 'posh' county, whose inhabitants speak in a 'Queen's English' accent. However, in my experience, the use of 'Estuary' English – a halfway house between cockney and standard English – is more common; and, also contrary to popular belief, very few people in Hampshire use a west country *oo arr* accent or dialect!

In the early 19th century, people living in rural south-west Hampshire, particularly the New Forest, which is just a stone's throw from Southampton, spoke a dialect which is now rarely heard. You can still find traces of words peculiar to the area, and the accent itself has changed little, but nowadays you're not likely to hear someone ask, *'Wair did ur cum vrom?'* ('Where did she come from?'), *'Bist dhee gwein too?'* ('Are you going, too?') or *'Haih, loo see, dhaier's a scuggee muggings zittin on l' gaalay-baagur!'* (Look, see, there's a squirrel sitting on the scarecrow')!

Sadly, along with many other local dialects around the British Isles, the use of a Hampshire dialect has steadily decreased as the population has became more mobile over the past 75 years. So the following glossary is a selection of words taken from what older local Southampton people either remember or still occasionally use, and from a collection of New Forester's dialect recorded around the turn of the last century.

A

Aaeel – ale
Aardinury – ordinary
Aardur – order
Aarkurd – awkward
Adhurt – across
Ad'n – had not
Aess – to ask, asked
Aij – edge
Aist – east
Ait – eat
Avert – across
Avoarhaand – before the event
Avroze – frozen, icy (of weather or conditions)
Awaaee – away

B

Baakay – tobacco
Baif – beef
Bailey – a bailiff
Baird – beard
Blakdhaarn – sloe bush (sloes are used to make a type of gin)
Blather – a fuss, uproar
Blood-turnip – beetroot
Bob – shilling
Bobbeen – robin
Boouth – both
Butturvloi – butterfly

C

Caark – cork
Caas'n or caint – can't
Chaik – cheek
Chawbacon – an unsophisticated person; a bumpkin or yokel
Childaag – chilblain
Chimblay, chimlay – chimney
Chiselbob – woodlouse
Cruncheon – informal evening meal
Claak – clock

Cockleert – cock-crow, daybreak
Coos'n, or coosint – could not
Cordner – more properly cordwainer; a shoemaker
Craitur – creature
Cuttay – wren

D

Daag – dog
Daid – dead
Deich – ditch
Dhaier – there
Dhaiuf – thief
Dheen – thin
Dhetzh – thatch
Dhum – thumb
Dipchick – a moorhen
Dirn – doorframe
Dishwasher – wagtail
Draap – drop
Driin – drain

E

Eier – higher
Eirun – iron

Emmet – ant
En – him
Enny wen – at any time
Er – ever
Ess – ass

F

Feesh – fish
Feller – fellow, chap
Figgety pudden – plum-pudding, the forerunner of Christmas Pudding
Fuzz buzz – traveller's joy

G

Gaaeet – gale
Gaalay-baagur (or gallibagger) – scarecrow
Gaun – dress
Gawermush – policeman
Gev – given
Goosegogs – gooseberries
Gowk – cuckoo
Gress – grass
Grunt – grumble
Gwein – part, going

H

Haalur – hollow
Haarn – horn
Happen – maybe
Heidin – hiding, thrashing
Herd – hard
Heth – heath
Hij – hedge
Hooum – home
Hoss, has – horse
Hous – house
Houzinz – houses

I

I'll count – I suppose, I concede
I'll own – I admit, I acknowledge,
I'll own up to
In – him
Insek – insect

J

Jillay staak – gilliflower (type of
carnation)
Jist – just

Joaay – a threepenny-bit
Job – difficulty
Joppety-joppety – in a state of
nervous anxiety, jittery

K

Kees – kiss
Kep – kept
Kiddil – kettle
Kiwur – cover
Kushti – good

L

Laeun – lane
Laif – leaf
Laiv – leave
Leat – a stream
Leik – such as
Lid – lead
Lug – pole or perch

M

Maaeed – girl
Mallyshag – caterpillar
Mazed – crazy, mad, mentally

unbalanced

Meind – remember
Mid'n – might not
Mimray – memory
Moak – donkey
Mommet – a scarecrow
Mump – stroll, wander
Muss'n – must not

N

Naist – nest
Nammet – lunch, usually taken by a labourer to eat at his place of work
Niwur – never
Noad – knew, known
Nog – chunk of wood
Nudhin – nothing
Nus – nurse

O

Oap – hope
Ollay – holly
Ood – wood
Ool – wool
Oolln – woollen

Oomun – woman

P

Paakit – pocket
Pait – peat
Pinchfart – mean, tight
Pinnee – pinafore
Plaaee – play
Plaes – place
Plag – plague
Poodin – pudding
Pook – heap of hay
Pus – purse
Pyooit – lapwing

Q

Quag – bog or marshy area
Qwair – queer
Qweiut – quiet
Qwid – cud

R

Raabit – rabbit
Raaeel – rail
Raaeen – rain

Randy – rustic celebration, often for a wedding or harvest
Rayed – dressed
Routle – to rummage (like a pig in straw)
Ruchtee – saddle-chain for a cart
Ruff – roof

S

Scraich – screech
Scuggee muggings – squirrel
Shrammed – frozen or cold to the bone

Hampshire Hog (or 'ampshire 'og) was used in jest to describe a Hampshire person, the county being famous for 'a fine breed of hogs, and the excellency of the bacon made there'! CREATIVE COMMONS

Shuffler – man employed in a farmyard
Smellfox – anemone
Smert – smart
Snag – sloe
Snoa – do you know
Sowbugs – woodlice
Speiur – spire
Spreathed – red raw, rough – usually of hands
Squeiur – squire
Staarlin – starling
Stook – stack of twelve sheaves of wheat or similar in a field
Strickle – block upon which a blade, usually a scythe or sickle, was sharpened
Stroy – destroy, kill off
Sucker – young colt
Swait – sweet

T

Taablish – fairly well
Taieh – teach
Tallow – animal fat used to make soap and candles

Tedn't – it isn't
Teit – tight
Tell – count
Tetchy – irritable
Tiddee – potato
Tithe – tax levied on crops and cattle, specifically one-tenth
Toordz – towards
Tooud – toad, and told
Traaeen – train
Trash – thrush
Trivet – tripod of iron for holding cooking vessels over the fire
Turmit (and turxnit) – turnip or occasionally swede
Tut-work – piece-work, paid for by the number of units produced

U

Un – him
Unrayed – undressed
Ur – her, them, or

V

Vaardin – farthing

Vaes, vaaees – face
Vaidhur – father
Vaist – feast
Vat – fat
Vaul – fall, veil, fell
Veeld – field
Veeoo – few
Veesh – fish
Veier – fire
Veilit – violet
Vellur – fellow
Voar – afore, before
Voul – fowl
Vrog – frog
Vromt – from
Vuirn – fern
Vurrur – furrow

W

Waaeet – weight
Waal – well
Wait – wheat
Wedher – castrated ram
Wet – weight
Wik – week

Wikkur – neigh, the noise a horse makes

Winker – child who seeks in 'heidee-hoop'

Winsh – wench, girl

Woar – worn

Wops – wasp

Wuird – word

Wuts – oats

Y

Yaalur – yellow

Yaandur – yonder

Yaaprun – apron

Yaas – yes

Yaeker – acorn

Yaffle – green woodpecker

Yardstack – stack of grain heaves waiting to be threshed

Yeer – here, and ear

Yoa – ewe

Yoorn – yours

Yungin – young one, youngster

Z

Zaaeem – same

Zaik – seek

Zaim – seem

Zault – salt

Zbeidur – spider

Zillur – cellar

Zizurz – scissors

Zooner – rather

Zooud – sold

HUMOUR

FUNNIES FROM THE STREETS OF SOUTHAMPTON

A group of freshers at Southampton University, who had just started their psychology course, were attending one of their first seminars. The topic was emotional extremes.

'Let's begin by discussing some contrasts,' said the tutor. He pointed to a student in the front row. *'What is the opposite of joy?'*

The student thought about it briefly, then answered, *'Sadness.'*

The tutor asked another student, *'What is the opposite of depression?'* She paused then said, *'Elation.'*

'And you,' the tutor said to another student sitting at the back, *'What about the opposite of woe?'*

The student thought for a moment, then replied, *'Um, I believe that would be "giddy up"!'*

A Southampton man walks past a pet shop in town. There's a sign in the window that says TALKING DOG FOR SALE.

The man doesn't believe it, but he's curious and so goes into the shop. He sees a dog, walks up to it and says, 'Hello, how's it going?'

The dog says, *'All right, mate. How are you?'*

The man says, *'You can really talk!'*

The dog says, *'That's right, mate.'*

The man says, 'So what is it like being a talking dog?'

The dog says, 'Well, I've lived a great life. I rescued avalanche victims in the Alps. I worked as a drug-sniffing dog for the FBI, and now I read to people in an old folks' home five days a week.'

The man is absolutely amazed. He turns to the owner of the pet shop and says, 'By Jove! Why would you sell a dog like this?'

The pet shop owner says, 'Because he's a damn liar! He never did ANY of those things.'

....

What do you get if you cross Portsmouth FC with an OXO cube? A LAUGHING STOCK.

....

A Southampton labourer shouted up to his roofer mate on top of an old terraced house, saying, 'Don't start climbing down this ladder, Bert.'

'Why not?' Bert called back.

'Cos I moved it five minutes ago!' replied his mate.

....

The president of the Southampton Vegetarian Society really couldn't control himself any more. He simply had to try some pork, just to see what it tasted like. So one day he told his members he was going away for a short break. He left town and headed to a restaurant in Eastleigh. He sat down, ordered a roasted pig, and waited impatiently for his treat. After only a few minutes, he heard someone call his name, and, to his horror, he saw one of his members walking towards him. At exactly the same moment, the waiter arrived at his table, with a huge platter, holding a whole roasted pig with an apple in its mouth. 'Isn't this place something?' said the president, thinking quickly. 'Look at the way they serve apples!'

A high-rise building was going up in Southampton, and three steel erectors sat on a girder having their lunch.

'Oh, no, not cream cheese and walnut again,' said Jim, the first one. *'If I get the same again tomorrow, I'll jump off the girder.'*

Harry opened his packet. *'Oh, no, not a Caesar salad with salami and lettuce on rye,'* he said. *'If I get the same again tomorrow, I'll jump off too.'*

Orson, the third man, opened his lunch. *'Oh, no, not another potato sandwich,'* he said. *'If I get the same again tomorrow, I'll follow you two off the girder.'*

The next day, Jim got cream cheese and walnut. Without delay, he jumped. Harry saw he had Caesar salad with salami and lettuce on rye and, with a wild cry, he leapt too. Then the third man, Orson, opened his lunchbox. *'Oh, no,'* he said. *'Potato sandwiches.'* And he too jumped.

The foreman, who had overheard their conversation, reported what had happened, and the funerals were held together.

'If only I'd known,' sobbed Jim's wife. *'If only he'd said,'* wailed Harry's wife. *'I don't understand it at all,'* said Orson's wife. *'He always got his own sandwiches ready.'*

....

Wiltshire man: 'There's a place in the Isle of Wight that does some really nice milk…'
Hampshire man: 'Cowes?'
Wiltshire man: 'No, goat's I think.'

....

The nervous young batsman playing for Southampton CC was having a very bad day. In a quiet moment in the game, he muttered to the one of his team mates, *'Well, I suppose you've seen worse players.'*

There was no response, so he said it again: *'I guess you've seen worse players.'* His team mate looked at him and answered, *'I heard you the first time. I was just trying to think…'*

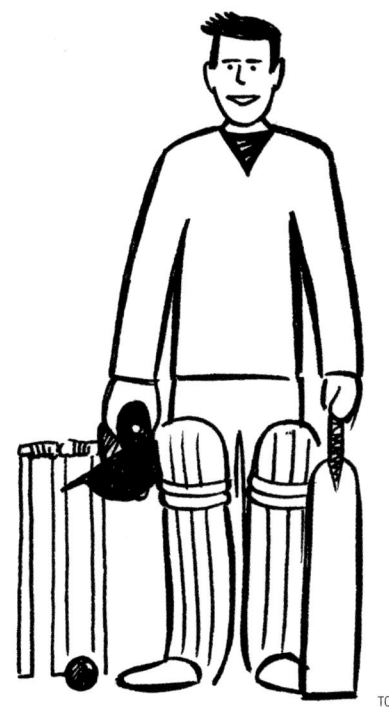

TOB

There's a man in Southampton who claims to have invented a game that's 'a bit like' cricket; what he doesn't realise is Hampshire County Cricket Club's been playing it for years.

....

At a pub in Southampton, a newcomer asked a local man, 'Have you lived here all your life?'

The old man took a sip of his ale and, after a long pause, replied, 'Don't know yet!'

....

A Southampton couple walked past a swanky new restaurant in Ocean Village. 'Did you smell that food?' the woman asked. 'Wonderful!'

Being the kind-hearted, generous man that he was, her husband thought, 'What the hell, I'll treat her!' So they walked past it a second time.

RECIPES

TASTY TREATS FROM SOUTHAMPTON

Solid Syllabub

**A Victorian dessert recipe
from the Isle of Wight.**

iStock

See **page 28** for recipe

Hampshire Friar's Omelette

Joan Ransley

I couldn't get to the bottom of why this was specifically called a 'Hampshire' Friar's omelette but was intrigued enough to try it; gosh, those Hampshire Friars had a good palette - *yummy!*

INGREDIENTS:

4 good-sized cooking apples

50gm sugar

Grated rind and flesh of 1 lemon

4 tablespoons breadcrumbs

85g butter

4 egg yolks

Cloves or nutmeg to flavour

PREPARATION:

1. Peel, core and slice apples, stew in a little water until soft. Allow to cool.

2. Cream butter and sugar together until light and fluffy.

3. Add chopped flesh and rind of lemon together with grated cloves or nutmeg to the creamed butter and sugar mix.

4. Grease a pie dish and sprinkle with about one tablespoon of breadcrumbs.

5. Beat yolks into the stewed apple in the saucepan.

6. Pour the apple into the pie dish. Dot the creamed butter mixture over the apples, cover with remaining breadcrumbs, and finish with pats of butter on top.

7. Bake in a moderate oven at 160°C for 1½ hours until the breadcrumbs are golden and the apples have set to a custard like consistency.

Poacher's Pie

Despite severe penalties, poachers in the New Forest were prepared to risk stealing game for this very tasty mixed pie!

iStock

INGREDIENTS:

1 medium onion, peeled and sliced

A little cooking oil

1400g mixed game – rabbit, venison, pheasant etc. – cubed and dusted with seasoned flour

110g mushrooms, sliced

½ teaspoon ground nutmeg

110g chestnuts, cooked and peeled

2 teaspoons fresh chopped parsley

Grated rind of half a lemon

Salt and black pepper

½pt pork stock

1 tablespoon of red wine or port (optional)

220gm short crust or puff pastry

Beaten egg to glaze

PREPARATION:

1. Set oven to 200°C.
2. Fry onion in oil until soft and mix with game, mushrooms, chestnuts, parsley, nutmeg, lemon rind and seasoning.
3. Place in a deep pie dish, inserting a pie funnel if necessary.
4. Mix the stock with the wine or port and pour just over half over the pie filling.
5. Roll out the pastry on a lightly floured surface into an oval slightly bigger than the pie dish.
6. Cut off a narrow strip, dampen with water and line the rim of the dish.
7. Dampen with water and place the remaining pastry over, sealing the edges well. Trim neatly and flute.
8. Make a steam hole in the centre and use any pastry trimmings to make leaves to decorate.
9. Brush with beaten egg and bake for 1 to 1½ hours, reducing temperature to 175°C after 30 minutes. Cover pie with foil if it browns too quickly.
10. When cooked, heat the remaining stock and top up the pie if necessary. Serve with new potatoes and a selection of vegetables.
Serves 4–6.

Solid Syllabub

INGREDIENTS:

½ **pint** medium sherry

100g sugar

1pt double cream

A little grated nutmeg

Rind and juice of a lemon or orange, according to your preference

PREPARATION:

1. Pour the sherry into a bowl and grate the lemon rind finely into the sherry.

2. In a separate bowl pour the lemon juice over the sugar and stir well.

3. Add to the sherry and continue to stir until the sugar has dissolved.

4. Whip the cream until it stands up in soft peaks and then fold into the sherry mixture.

5. Spoon into four sundae glasses and sprinkle the tops lightly with nutmeg and a sprinkle of orange or lemon rind.

SHOCKING SOUTHAMPTON

RETRIBUTION FOR A BULLY

Black American **Robert Fisher**, aged 17, was charged at Southampton Magistrates' Court with the murder of **John Macaulay**, a mate on board the vessel Voyageur. According to evidence given by a Russian sailor, Fisher joined the ship in Richmond, USA in 1881, sailing for Pernambuco, in South America. Throughout the voyage Fisher was persistently bullied and teased by the captain and Macaulay, and made to complete tasks that should have been done by the older sailors.

Finally, soon after midnight on 20 December, his temper gave way. He'd accidentally dropped a pot of grease on deck and made a mess, after which an argument led to a struggle, and Fisher used a sheath knife (which he was using to clear up the grease) to stab his long-time tormentor. Macaulay died within just a few minutes and was buried at sea.

ISTOCK

When questioned about what he'd done, Fisher at first said that he'd been aloft, scraping the mast, and that the knife must have fallen from his pocket!

At Winchester Assizes on 19 May, the jury found Fisher guilty of manslaughter, but strongly recommended that he be shown mercy on account of his age and the amount of provocation he'd been subjected to. The judge accordingly gave him one month's imprisonment, during which he said he hoped Fisher's friends 'could arrange for his future well-being'.

MARRY ME OR DIE!

Abraham Baker (29) was brought before Southampton magistrates on 16 October 1855, charged with the wilful murder of **Naomi Kingswell**. They'd worked as footman and housemaid for the Reverend Poynder and his family of Moira Place,

iSTOCK

Southampton. On 14 October he shot her dead in the kitchen, as a result of what is believed to be unrequited love. Naomi had told Abraham that she had absolutely no interest in him. Investigations found a new gold wedding ring in his wallet, along with a letter that he'd written to his parents on the morning of the murder.

The letter began *'This may be the last time I shall have to write to you…'* He was found guilty at Winchester Assizes, and while he was waiting to be executed he confessed that he'd been 'driven wild with jealousy' by her 'womanish and teasing coquetry'. He was hanged on 8 January 1856.

KEY AND CLOTHES HELP IDENTIFY BODY

A sales representative for the Wolf's Head oil company in Southampton, **Vivian Messiter**, aged 57, was found dead on the floor of his garage in Grove Street. His body had already started to rot and rats had almost completely eaten his face away, so it was only possible to identify him from his clothes and from a door key found in his pocket. Identification was carried out by **Mr Parrot** of Carlton Road, Messiter's landlord. The last time he had been seen alive was when he left his lodgings on 30 October 1928. At first it was thought that he'd died from a gunshot wound, but the home office pathologist carried out a post-mortem and found that he'd been hit over the head with a hammer or a similar sort of heavy blunt instrument. Enquiries led the police to **William Thomas**, a motor mechanic, otherwise known as **William Podmore**, who had a long criminal record.

He was due to serve six months in gaol for a robbery in Manchester, followed by a similar sentence for stealing wage packets in Wiltshire.

When he was released from these sentences on 17 December 1929, he was swiftly re-arrested and charged with Messiter's murder. Evidence pointed to the fact that he'd written fictitious receipts for sales of oil to non-existent companies. Messiter, who'd just taken on Podmore the week before his death, paid the fake receipts and then discovered his new employee's fraudulent behaviour. After an argument, Podmore killed him, stole his gold dress watch, tore the receipts from the receipt book and disappeared. Pleading not guilty, and claiming he knew 'nothing about it', he was tried at Winchester Assizes on 3 March 1930, found guilty, and hanged at Winchester on 28 April.

HAMMERED TO DEATH WHILE SLEEPING

On 8 March 1913, 17-year-old **Harry Blaker** was tried at Winchester Assizes and found guilty of murdering his grandfather, **Frederick Ridges** (59),

SHUTTERSTOCK/CHANTAL DE BRUIJNE

a widower of Southampton. They had lived together for about 14 years until, after a disagreement, Blaker struck his grandfather with a hammer while he was asleep. The defence argued that Harry was mentally defective and in returning their verdict the jury recommended he be shown mercy.

The judge passed a sentence of death, but this was later changed to detention during His Majesty's pleasure.

A CRIME OF PASSION!

George Broomfield, a butler at a house near Alresford, died in South Hampshire Infirmary in Southampton. Two days before that, **Frederick Colburne**, who lived at Shirley Common, went to buy some beer, while his wife **Caroline**, six months pregnant, was preparing an evening meal. Caroline had been a lady's maid at the same house as Broomfield. While her husband was out, Broomfield visited, apparently to pay his respects, but in fact his intention was to try to persuade her to run away with him to America.

When Mr Colburne returned, he found to his horror that Broomfield had shot Caroline dead and then turned the pistol on himself. He said that he'd done it from love and that

CREATIVE COMMONS

nobody could possibly know the pain he'd suffered over the past nine months since she'd married Mr Colburne. When he was admitted to the hospital, he told the surgeon that several years earlier he'd been shot in the head and since then had suffered from fits of mental derangement. After lingering in agony for two days, he died.

This version of events is taken from the Daily News. Interestingly, according to other newspapers, Broomfield made a full recovery, was tried at Winchester Assizes for wilful murder on 17 July 1865, found guilty, and sentenced to be hanged. Then, as now, you can't always believe what you read in the papers.

LOCAL NAMES

If you were to ask a random selection of Sotonians what names are most often associated with Soton, it's not surprising that, as the town has such a long and rich seafaring heritage, two that are frequently mentioned are MAYFLOWER and TITANIC.

MAYFLOWER

In 1620, the Pilgrim Fathers departed from Southampton for America in their ships, Mayflower and Speedwell. The Pilgrims chartered the Mayflower to sail to the 'New World' to escape religious oppression in England, and also bought a smaller boat, the Speedwell, built in Southampton, to use permanently when they reached America.

The Mayflower iSTOCK

The Speedwell and the Mayflower eventually sailed from Southampton for the New World on 15 August 1620. However, the Speedwell began to leak and was finally deemed too unreliable to attempt the crossing. All the personnel and stores were transferred to Mayflower, which eventually left England on 6 September 1620 with 102 passengers, as well as at least two dogs. Two people died during the trip and one baby was born, who was named Oceanus Hopkins! After a gruelling 66-day journey, they landed in Cape Cod on 9 November 1620. Today Mayflower Park and the Mayflower memorial in Southampton commemorate their departure from England's shores. Southampton is also looking forward to commemorating the 400th anniversary of the Pilgrim Fathers leaving the city in 2020.

TITANIC

In 1912, a job aboard the mighty passenger liner, Titanic, was a dream come true for the men of this English port, offering three square meals a day and lodgings for the night at a time of severe hardship.

When Titanic set off from Southampton docks on her fateful maiden voyage to New York on 10 April 1912, the people of the city proudly cheered her off. Five days later – on 15 April – the luxury passenger liner sank about

Titanic stamp iStock

375 miles south of Newfoundland, Canada, after hitting an iceberg, killing more than 1,500 people, 549 of them Southampton residents.

The first news of the sinking was posted in the window of a local newspaper just hours after the disaster, but no one believed it at first. Photographs at the time show anxious relatives gathering around the names of the dead posted outside the offices of the Titanic's owners, the White Star

Line, where a small black plaque on the now-shabby building marks the spot. Southampton was plunged into mourning and many of the victims' families were left in poverty.

The city pulled together to raise money for the bereaved families and in the months after the disaster, every concert and church fete was turned into a Titanic fundraiser. One of the fatalities, Sidney Sedunary, a steward, had been carrying a pocket watch which stopped at 1.50am – about half an hour before the Titanic sank. A few days later, his body was hauled from the water by a rescue ship and the watch, which now takes pride of place in Southampton's SeaCity museum, was found in his pocket.

Titanic Engineers Memorial Southampton

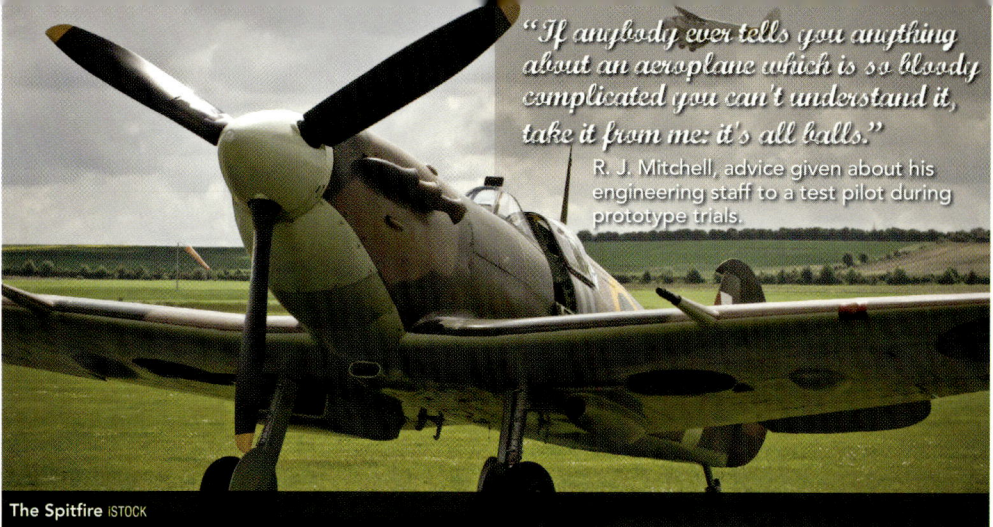

"If anybody ever tells you anything about an aeroplane which is so bloody complicated you can't understand it, take it from me: it's all balls."

R. J. Mitchell, advice given about his engineering staff to a test pilot during prototype trials.

The Spitfire iSTOCK

SPITFIRE

Another name associated with the city is the Spitfire, which was designed by **Reginald Joseph Mitchell** (1895-1937), a British aeronautical engineer, working for Supermarine of Southampton. Between 1920 and 1936 he designed many aircraft, including light aircraft, fighters, bombers and flying boats, but is best remembered for his work on a series of racing aircraft, culminating in the iconic World War II fighter, the **Supermarine Spitfire**.

The first prototype Spitfire, serial number K5054, flew for the first time on 5 March 1936 at Eastleigh, just outside Southampton. In later tests it reached 349 mph, and even before the prototype had completed its official trials the RAF ordered 310 production Spitfires. Mitchell's design was so sound that the Spitfire was continually improved throughout the war and over 22,000 Spitfires and derivatives were built. Mitchell was depicted in the film The First of the Few.

WALKS

EXPLORE SOUTHAMPTON'S MARITIME HISTORY AND TAKE A STROLL IN THE PARK!

This walk takes you through all five of Southampton's Centre Parks. You'll see some of the city's memorials, and if you choose, can visit SeaCity, Southampton's maritime museum and the City Art Gallery.

Distance: 1.5miles/2.5km
Time: without visits 30 mins; with visits to SeaCity or the gallery, and stopping to admire memorials, half a day (or more).

Starting from the Civic Centre, follow the road around to the right, past the clock tower and SeaCity museum. Cross Above Bar Street heading towards Cumberland Road, and enter Watts Park on your left. Immediately in front of you is the sculpture *'Enclosure'* by **Paul De Monchaux** (2000), commissioned under the heritage

Isaac Watts statue iSTOCK

lottery fund scheme. Continuing to the centre of the park you'll find a statue to its namesake, the famous author, educator, philosopher and hymn writer Isaac Watts. His well-known hymn *'O God, our help in ages past'* echoes across the park from the Civic Centre clock tower at 8.00 am, noon and 4.00 pm!

Turn east from Watts' statue and head towards the impressive Cenotaph, designed by **Edwin Lutyens** and added in 1920. From there, leave the park turning left towards Cumberland Road.

Cross Above Bar Street into Andrews (East) Park. Immediately opposite is a large memorial to the Engineer Officers of the Titanic,

Detail of Titanic Engineer Memorial

none of whom survived. Unveiled in 1914, the memorial is constructed of Aberdeen granite and surmounted by a seven foot high angel.

This park has the most trees, shrubs, rose beds, plants, spring and summer bulbs, bedding, ferns, grasses and bamboos of the Central Parks. It has a wide range of Alpine plants in the 1930s-built rock garden. It is typical of the Victorian's love of plants brought in from all over the Empire and beyond. Enjoy strolling southwards towards Palmerston Park.

Palmerston Park is densely planted with mainly acidic soil loving plants such as camellias, rhododendrons, azaleas, magnolias and witch hazels. You will find a statue of former Prime Minster the 3rd Viscount Palmerston, MP for South Hampshire for many years. It stands seven feet high on its plinth and is made of white marble and granite. The Bandstand was

Palmerston Park

built as a result of public demand and completed in 1999. The original cast iron bandstand, from 1885, was further north in the park and removed in 1940 as a result of bomb damage. Continuing southward, leave Palmerston Park and cross Pound Tree Road into Houndwell Park.

Houndwell Park has a large all-ability play area, opened 2013, very popular with Southampton's younger residents! Continue south down the lime tree avenue to the **William Chamberlayne Gas Column**, a 50 foot high fluted Doric column, cast in iron. It was built as a tribute to **William Chamberlayne**, MP for the town 1818-1829.

Leave the park and turn left, crossing the road into **Hoglands Park**, the 'village green' of Central Park's, with its cricket squares and informal 'kick-about' area in relaxed parkland. Areas around the park's boundaries are planted and managed with native plants to encourage wildlife. In the centre is the popular skatepark. The Pavilion houses a drop-in centre

Gas Column
Shutterstock/BasPhoto

for young people to meet, talk and learn IT skills. The buildings were painted by local street artists, adding to the appeal for younger park visitors. The park has been used for many events, including Tour of Britain cycle race finish, Sport Relief, circuses, etc.

From the centre of the park take the diagonal path in a north-westerly direction, straight back through Palmerston Park, and on to Above Bar Street. To visit the City Art Gallery, continue north and turn left into Commercial Road.

SOUTHAMPTON OLD TOWN WALK

Distance: 1.25 miles
Time: Approx one hour
Some steps so unsuitable for wheelchairs

Enter the walled town through the Bargate's grand entrance, and trace the footsteps of generations of townspeople and visitors who came to Southampton to trade or sail from its port. Built about 1180, Bargate kept out intruders and impressed visitors. Continue down Bargate Street, the town walls to your left. These were first built to defend the town from attack by land, and then extended to protect it from seaborne enemies, following the French raid of 1338.

On the corner is **Arundel Tower**. Continue left down Western Esplanade and you will come to **Catchcold Tower**, so called because if you were a raider with plans to attack the medieval town, the soldiers with guns posted there would "catch you cold".

Tudor House iSTOCK

Continuing along the wall you'll come to **Castle Vault**, used to store the King's valuable goods, including wine from Bordeaux. Medieval merchants had to pay him one in every 10 barrels of wine they imported, as tax.

A little further on, where the wall starts again, is a plaque where Southampton Castle once stood. Built after the Norman conquest of 1066, the King and his court stayed here on their way to France. In medieval times, this area was a bustling waterfront lined with houses of wealthy merchants. After the French Raid the merchants were forced to move and the walls of their houses were blocked up to create the town walls. You can still see outlines of medieval doorways and windows.

City walls at night

Continue to the Arcades. In October 1338, 50 ships brought French and Genoese raiders to storm the town. They attacked and killed residents, looted possessions and set fire to buildings. King Edward II was furious about the raid (and the loss of his wine!) and commanded a wall to be built against future attacks. Merchants were forced to block up the entrances to their quayside warehouses to build the defensive arcades you see today.

One arcade leads up steps to **Blue Anchor Lane**, the route from the medieval quayside into town and the market in **St Michael's Square**. Proceed to St Michael's Square. Now dominated by the iconic **Tudor House**, this square was once the location of Westgate Hall. Wool was stored upstairs, and a fish market was held beneath. In 1634 the hall was dismantled and rebuilt next to Westgate.

Turn right from **Blue Anchor Lane** into **Bugle Street** and then right again into **Westgate Street**. The Westgate on your left was built following the French Raid of 1338. In 1415 Henry V and his army departed through here on their way to victory at Agincourt, and sailors and passengers of the Mayflower and the Speedwell passed through Westgate on their way to America in 1620.

Continue on to **Western Esplanade** and follow the wall around to Town Quay. During the 1400s the **Wool House** was

God's House Tower SHUTTERSTOCK

built to store wool (the town's largest export) right on the quayside. Continue to the corner of High Street and what remains of **Watergate**. In 1476, Italian ships tied up to unload Mediterranean wines, dried fruits, spices and silks; Watergate resonated with voices of foreign sailors passing through the main entrance into town.

From here turn right along **Winkle Street** to **God's House Tower**, which provided formidable defence for the medieval town. Turn up Back of the Walls to **Friary Gate**. Franciscan friars settled here in 1224. They preached

The Wool House SHUTTERSTOCK/BASPHOTO

and cared for the poor, sick, aged and outcast, and also introduced a piped water supply to the town – just beyond the wall you can still see where the town ditch ran down to the shore near God's House Tower. A sluice gate there allowed the ditch to fill with water at high tide, to help defend the town. Continue along Back of the Walls toward **East Street** and the **Bargate**.

At **Bernard Street** turn left toward the **High Street** and visit the **church of Holy Rood**, now a memorial to merchant seamen. Continue up the High Street, turn right into **East Street** then left through the shopping centre to York Way. In 1202, King John gave £100 to "close the town" and build a line of defences to protect its people. The North Wall was the first to be built and links Bargate to Eastgate. **York Gate** was cut into the wall in 1769. Go up the steps, turn right and then left to arrive back at Bargate.

Holy Rood Church SHUTTERSTOCK/IAN GRAINGER

GHOSTLY LEGIONS

Near Bitterne Manor, close to the Northam Bridge that crosses the River Itchen, there's a notorious bend in the road, where sightings of ghostly Roman legionaries have been reported over the years. There was once a Roman settlement called Clausentum located here, which was home to Roman legions until around AD 410; single and large groups of ghostly figures have been seen on the bend, ignoring the traffic bearing down on them. Apparently, sightings were particularly frequent in the 1950s when a new bridge was being built across the river. Perhaps the soldiers were unhappy at being disturbed!

Ghostly Romans SHUTTERSTOCK/MORPHART CREATION

HOST OF GHOSTS!

The Red Lion, in the High Street, was built in 1148 and is supposed to be the most haunted pub in Southampton, with allegedly up to 21 ghosts! Bar staff and regular visitors report having seen an old lady drifting behind the bar; she's believed to be the ghost of a barmaid from many years ago who died when she fell down the cellar steps. However, the most frequently reported sighting is that of three men leaving the pub together.

In 1415, immediately before King Henry V left from Southampton for the Battle of Agincourt, the three ringleaders of the 'Southampton Plot' against the king – Richard, Earl of Cambridge, Henry Scrope, 3rd Baron Scrope of Masham and Sir Thomas Grey of Heaton – were tried and found guilty of high treason, before being executed outside the Bargate. The ghostly procession is thought to be the three men walking towards the gallows.

The Red Lion Pub

TUDOR GHOSTS

Southampton's most important historic building, Tudor House, reveals over 800 years of history in the heart of the Old Town. The timber-framed building facing St Michael's Square was built in the late 15th century, with King John's Palace, an adjacent Norman house accessible from Tudor House Garden, dating back a further 300 years. One of Southampton's most haunted locations, the Tudor House has seen many reports of ghosts. A lot of these have come from staff and members of the public who have seen, heard or felt a presence in the Green Room.

Dogs refuse to enter this room and ghostly apparitions are regularly witnessed. Dark, ominous figures have been seen all around the house and an unearthly presence is felt throughout. In the Georgian room on the upper floors people have reported

Tudor street at night

being touched and strange orbs have been seen on visitors' cameras. Unexplained footsteps and bangs that can't be located are also regularly heard.

EAST WELLOW

A ghostly figure can be seen in St Margaret's Church, thought to be that of Florence Nightingale who is buried in the graveyard and who attended the church for many years. At midnight on New Year's Eve, a coach-and-four can be seen driving from Embley Park to St Margaret's Church. The ghost of Colonel William Morton has been seen walking from the site of the old manor to the churchyard. He was a native of the village and was one of the people who signed Charles I's death warrant.

THE HAUNTED HOTEL

Built in the 1870s, the South Western Hotel's fame came from hosting the high society passengers before their fateful voyage aboard RMS Titanic in 1912. The hotel looks directly out over the docks, where the Titanic would have been an imposing sight for the guests. Many of the hotel's residents claim to have seen the apparition of a man wandering through one of the corridors. He appears to be moving very fast and is desperate about something. He usually appears close to Room 667, and a cry of pain has also often been heard in this area. The story goes that on the evening of 15 November 1931, the hotel porter heard what he thought to be the sound of a gunshot, so used his key to go into Room 667.

He was faced with what he believed to be two dead bodies. Investigations discovered that the couple apparently had a suicide pact, yet the woman survived. Thinking that that his lover had been shot dead, the man – a Mr Roland Draper – turned the gun on himself, dying instantly. However, having denied their wishes to be together it's thought that Mr Draper has since been frantically roaming the corridor looking for his lover.

South Western House

The building is no longer a hotel; it's now known as South Western House and contains a variety of apartments. I wonder whether Mr Draper is still in evidence?

TOTTON

Testwood House was once a hunting lodge used by Henry VIII. It has a ghostly dog and the sounds of a spirit-driven coach as well as more random ghosts such as faces peering from windows and the inexplicable rattling of doors. It is believed the cook was murdered by another member of staff at the house and that her ghost is still present. An apparition of a male figure has also been reported on several occasions.

GHOST NURSE AT NETLEY

A Grey Lady often appeared to patients at the Royal Victoria Military Hospital, which took causalities from the Boer War and both world wars. Apparently,

SHUTTERSTOCK/LARIO TUS

the apparition would appear at the bedsides of patients who died shortly afterwards. She is believed to have been a Crimean War nurse, although recent investigations have revealed that a nursing sister once threw herself from an upper floor, having poisoned her lover on finding him with his arm around another lady. As well as at dying patients' bedsides the Grey Lady was often seen along the extremely long downstairs corridor. An exorcism was held in 1951, but to no avail as the lady continued to appear. Eventually, the hospital was demolished in 1966, leaving just the chapel, and the last sighting of the ghost was by a demolition contractor, who saw her at a ward entrance.

REVERSE REINCARNATION?

In St Olave's Church on the Isle of Wight an oak effigy of Edward Estur, a crusader, rests in the sanctuary with a toy dog at his feet. He belonged to the family who founded the church

The chapel is all that remains of the Royal Victoria Military Hospital iSTOCK

in 1292. Hundreds of years later, a farmer's daughter called Lucy Lightfoot became obsessed with the effigy and visited the church every day to spend time with him. She was in the church in 1831 when a storm hit the island, followed by an eclipse of the sun. Later that day a farmer passed the church and found Lucy's horse sweating and distressed. Lucy had vanished and was never found. A jewel and lodestone set in the hilt of the crusader's iron dagger had also disappeared. More than 30 years later it was discovered that Edward had fought in the Holy Land in the 14th century accompanied by Lucy Lightfoot of Carisbrook. Experts believe a reincarnation in reverse may have happened – a time warp triggered by the storm and eclipse!

BILLINGHAM MANOR

A scent of Madonna lilies accompanies the appearance of the ghost of Billingham Manor on the Isle of Wight, whose life ended when he was killed in a duel concerning a Miss Legh. It has also been reported that a secret panel in the dining room was pushed open to reveal an apparition of the severed head of Charles I – it then slowly faded away. Charles was held captive at Carisbrooke Castle on the island and the Worsleys, who owned Billingham, devised a plot to free him.

Carisbrooke Castle

OUT AND ABOUT IN SOUTHAMPTON

Maritime Festival

There really is something for everyone at Southampton Maritime Festival, a two-day event held in August to celebrate the city's wartime and maritime history. It's Southampton's largest historical event, attracting thousands of visitors every year. This is a chance to explore historic ships, fishing boats, yachts and tugs, including the National Historic Fleet vessels HMS Medusa, ST Challenge, and SS Shieldhall. Visitors can board the ships and learn all about their role in the world wars. The Association of Dunkirk Little Ships, a charity dedicated to restoring ships that took part in Operation Dynamo in 1940, also provides vessels, as well as traditional boat-building demonstrations to educate the public about their work.

SS Shieldhall

On land, there are plenty of attractions on all aspects of Southampton's wider wartime history. The Historical Diving Society provides demonstrations with heavy 'hard hat' diving gear, giving guests a unique insight into diving in the 19th century, and there's even the chance to try them on yourself. There are exhibits of heritage buses, steam vehicles, and trams to enjoy, with free tours of the city's historic sites aboard an open-top bus. The Southampton Tourist Guides Association offers themed walks, including a tour around the dock all about the Titanic, which set sail from Southampton on 10 April 1912. The Ocean Cruise Terminal houses art and photography displays, craft stalls, and a variety of traders, while local historical associations hold stalls dedicated to subjects as diverse as archaeology, engineering and stamps.

Southampton Boat Show, held in September in one of Europe's largest marinas, is a boating enthusiast's dream. The event gathers together suppliers from all around the country to showcase an astounding variety of the latest and best products, with thousands of sail and power boats, yachts, dinghies and personal watercraft on display. Visitors of all ages and abilities can benefit from lots of free activities. The Try-A-Boat feature offers a chance to get out on the water in a wide selection of boats, whether you're a beginner after your

Southampton Boat Show SHUTTERSTOCK/JANE RIX

first taste of boating or a veteran keen to get a feel for a boat before buying. Younger visitors can have a go at dinghy sailing and paddle-boarding with Get Afloat, a free 90-minute session for 8-16-year-olds led by instructors. You can visit the Active Marina Experience, a series of workshops run by the Royal Yachting Association on shore and on the water, to pick up new techniques and get tips from experts. Or climb on board a 72-ft Ocean Race Yacht as part of a 12-strong team and take a thrilling ride around the Solent. You don't need to be experienced – just adventurous!

Southampton Boat Show iSTOCK

The show is also a great opportunity to meet like-minded people and exhibitors, have a chat and ask their advice on all aspects of boating. As well as the boats themselves, visitors will find every kind of equipment and service imaginable, from deck shoes and rigging to refrigeration and insurance. Since 1826, **Cowes Week** has been one of the most popular events in the British sporting calendar and attracts over 100,000 spectators annually. The iconic regatta, held in the Solent off Cowes on the Isle of Wight every August, mixes boat races with live entertainment and social activities. The 800 to 1,000 boats are divided into 40 classes, and races are held every day of the week. The Solent's infamously varied weather and sea conditions often make for exciting

Round the Island Boat Race, IoW iSTOCK

and unpredictable races! Watch the action from the Green or the Parade, or book a ringside seat aboard a spectator boat. Visitors can also stand between the Castle of the Royal Yacht Squadron and the cannons, closest to the starting line. The great thing about this event is that anyone can take part, with Olympic and professional sailors competing alongside amateurs.

A highlight is the annual **Round the Island Race**, a one-day yacht race around the Isle of Wight in which world-class sailors race against families and novices. Spectators can follow the race from various observation points along the course.

But it's not all about the boats. Along the shore you'll find plenty of pubs, restaurants and cafes, places to visit such as the Cowes Maritime Museum, and great entertainment happening throughout the week, including live music, street theatre, aerial displays and an outdoor cinema. Sailing taster sessions, run by youth charity UKSA, are open to all – you could even go one step further and try your hand at racing as well.

WHEN THE SAINTS GO MARCHING IN...

FOOTBALL - THE SAINTS

Southampton Football Club have played their football at the modern all-seater St Mary's Stadium since 2001, after spending 103 years at their former home, known fondly as 'The Dell', which in 1898 cost just £10,000 to build. Before that, the team's early matches were played on the local common, and were often interrupted by locals strolling across the pitch! Known as **'The Saints'**, the club was formed in 1885 as a church team – St Mary's Church of England Young Men's Association – and generally play in red and white stripes.

The Saints joined the Football League Third Division in 1920, which was split into South and North a year later. They were promoted into the Second Division and stayed there for 31 years. During World War II they spent a short time playing at Fratton Park, the home ground of their local rivals, Portsmouth FC, because a bomb had landed on The Dell, creating an 18-foot crater, damaging major water pipes and flooding the pitch.

Manager Ted Bates finally lifted the Saints to the First Division in 1966, but they then spent many years moving back and forward between the top two divisions. In 1976 Lawrie McMenemy famously took the Saints to Wembley where, as underdogs from Division Two, they beat favourites Manchester United to win the coveted FA Cup. McMenemy continued this success by taking Southampton FC into Division

St Mary's Stadium CREATIVE COMMONS

One, where they stayed for 27 years and were founder members of the modern Premier League that we know today.

Despite a short stint in Divisions Two and Three in recent times, Southampton FC were again promoted to the Premiership in 2012, and after a hugely successful season in 2013/14 they recently appointed the former Dutch International

Ronald Koeman as manager, ahead of the 2014/15 season. Many new players are being bought, and a new Saints team is being forged to compete once again in the top tier of English football. Maybe some new household names will emerge to compare with former notable players such as Alan Ball, Mick Channon, Peter Shilton, Kevin Keegan, Matthew Le Tissier, Alan Shearer, Theo Walcott and Gareth Bale, to name but a (very impressive) few!

England vs Sri Lanka CREATIVE COMMONS

CRICKET

Southampton's Ageas Bowl is the home of Hampshire Cricket – one of the 18 first-class cricketing counties in England and Wales. Established in 1863, the club has been home to some of the world legends of cricket over the years, including Shane Warne, the Australian spin bowler, West Indian fast bowler Malcolm Marshall, and England batsman Robin Smith, amongst many more.

These days, Hampshire can count internationally honoured players as well as some of the most exciting prospects in English cricket amongst its ranks. The team reached glory in 1961 and again in 1973 by winning the County Championship. However, the club has also won a very respectable 11 limited-overs titles; they created history in 2010 when they became the first British domestic side to win a Twenty20 Cup on home turf in front of a packed South Coast crowd of 25,000 supporters. And in 2012, they completed an historic double by winning the Friends Life T20.

The club play in three domestic competitions over the summer months of April to September – the LV= County Championship, the Royal London One-Day Cup, and the NatWest T20 Blast.

Twenty20 (T20) was introduced in 2003 to create a fast-paced form of the game which would be attractive to spectators at the ground and viewers on television. In a T20 game the two teams have a single innings each, restricted to a maximum of 20 overs. A game is completed in about three hours, much shorter than other forms of the game, and is closer to the timespan of many other popular team sports.

WATER SPORTS

As you'd expect from a coastal city, Southampton has a huge variety of water sports available, for novices or old sea dogs alike! From yachting or rowing, to sailing or windsailing, jet-skiing or motor-boating … you won't have far to go, either to participate or to watch.

Sailing iSTOCK

LOCAL HISTORY

THE EARLY STUFF!

Southampton has been a settlement for a very long time: gravel pits dug in the area have revealed many Stone Age tools; Bronze Age objects have been found on Southampton Common; and evidence of Iron Age buildings has also been found in and around the city centre.

The Romans are believed to have been here between AD 43 and 410. Archaeological evidence shows the site to have been an important Roman trading port, with some significant buildings and traces of a Roman Road on a line running from Bitterne Manor to Wickham. When the Romans left Britain, the Anglo-Saxons moved the centre of the town across the River Itchen to what is now the St Mary's area. The settlement was known

Viking boat iSTOCK

as Hamwic and/or Hamtun. By the middle of the 11th century, the area is described as South Hamtun by Anglo-Saxon Chroniclers. Excavations have revealed one of the best collections of Saxon artefacts in Europe, showing that Hamwic was a planned town and an important port that traded with the continent.

Between 700 and 1066, Viking raids on Southampton disrupted trade with the Continent and contributed to the reorganisation of Wessex, and important industries established in Hamwic were drawn further inland to new fortifications at Winchester, contributing to Hamwic's decline. Archaeological evidence shows 10th-century settlements and a defended enclosure in what was later to become the medieval walled town. The Viking King Canute the Great defeated the Anglo-Saxon King Ethelred the Unready in 1014 and was crowned in Southampton.

Following the Norman Conquest in 1066, Southampton's prosperity was assured when it became the major port of transit between Winchester (capital of England until the early 12th century) and Normandy, in France. The Domesday Book shows that Southampton already had distinct French and English quarters at the time of the Norman Conquest and that the King owned a number of properties.

Henry II, the first King of the House of Plantagenet, was a regular visitor to Southampton and established Southampton Castle, mainly as his own personal wine cellar! Surviving remains of 12th-century merchants' houses, such as King John's House and Canute's Palace, are evidence of the wealth that existed in Southampton during this period.

By the 13th century, the town was a leading port, involved in the trading

Bargate iSTOCK

of French wine and English wool. The Wool House was built in 1417 as a warehouse for the medieval wool trade with Flanders and Italy.

By 1173, the St Mary Magdalen leper hospital was established to the north of the town. St Julian's Hospital, otherwise known as God's House Hospital, was founded around 1196 by Gervase 'le Riche', and the Franciscan Friary was later built alongside God's House Hospital. Bowls was first played regularly on the green next to the hospital in 1299, which is the world's oldest surviving bowling green.

After the town was pillaged in 1338 by the French, the city's walls – parts of which date from 1175 – were extensively reinforced. However, with no money to build a full defensive wall, the townsfolk joined the outside walls of existing merchant houses together to form a defensive arrangement.

City wall iSTOCK

THE MIDDLE BIT!

During the Middle Ages, shipbuilding became an increasingly important industry and remained so for centuries. However, Southampton's economic fortunes fluctuated during the Tudor period. From 1492 to 1531, all exports of tin and lead were required to pass through Southampton. Trade with the Channel Islands increased and in 1554 the town was granted a monopoly on the export of wool to the Mediterranean and on the import of sweet wine. At other times during this period, the port was in decline, mainly because trade was shifting to London. Southampton was also a convenient port for the buccaneers who plundered Spanish ships in the English Channel and the Atlantic Ocean. Henry VIII's development of Hurst, Calshot, Cowes and Netley castles along Southampton Water and the Solent in about 1540 meant that Southampton was not so dependent on its fortifications.

Calshot Castle iSTOCK

The port was the original point of departure for the Pilgrim Fathers aboard the Mayflower in 1620. Since that time it has been the last port of call for millions of emigrants who left the Old World to start a new life in the USA, Australia, Canada, New Zealand, South Africa, Barbados and elsewhere.

In 1642, during the English Civil War, a Parliamentary garrison moved into Southampton to defend against seaborne attack from Royalist ships. A Royalist army advanced as far as Redbridge in March 1644 but were prevented from taking the town – the Battle of Cheriton removed the threat. In June 1664, the Black Death caused serious disruption to Southampton; by November 1666, 1,700 people had died.

Less than 80 years later, in 1740, thanks to the discovery of a spring of Chalybeate water, Southampton became a fashionable spa town, earning royal patronage which aided its prosperity and development. By the 1760s it had also become a popular area for sea bathing, despite the lack of a good beach! At West Quay, baths were built that filled and emptied with the flow of the tide, known as

Walls and Tudor merchant house ISTOCK

the Long Rooms, and there was a long promenade with views across the water to be enjoyed by spectators and bathers alike.

NOT THAT LONG AGO!

The Victorian era saw huge expansion in the town; the Southampton Docks Company was formed in 1835 and the first dock opened on 29 August 1842. The Royal Mail Steam Packet Company operated its services from Southampton, and the structural and economic development of the docks continued for the next few decades.

The railway link from Southampton to London was fully opened in May 1840, and by 1847 Southampton was also connected to Dorchester by rail. In 1866, a branch line extended the railway over the River Itchen at St Denys, passing through Bitterne and Woolston to Netley. With good transport links, Southampton became the emigrant station for North America and Australia, and in 1846 the Southampton Emigration and Shipping Company was formed, turning the town into '**The Gateway to the Empire'**.

Titanic – Gateway to the Empire

Cholera epidemics in 1848-49 and 1865, centred on the slums of the old medieval town, caused great concern; in 1894, the Borough Medical Officer of Health published a report on poverty in the town. Population density in the slums was recorded as 441.4 per acre until a slum clearance plan created new streets and a lodging house, St Michaels House, was opened in 1899. In 1914, at the outbreak of World War I, Southampton was designated No. 1 Military Embarkation Port; much of Southampton Common was taken over by the military and over eight million troops and their equipment departed for mainland Europe through the port. A steady flow of refugees, prisoners of war and over a million wounded came back to England through Southampton.

The period between the two world wars saw an increase in traffic, as the car and the tramways evolved. It became necessary to develop new routes around the Bargate as the central arch was too much of an obstruction. Several old buildings and part of the medieval walls were demolished on both sides of the Bargate, and in 1932 it was bypassed on its eastern side, and became an island when it was bypassed on its western side in 1938.

The Second World War hit Southampton particularly hard. Pockets of Georgian architecture remain, but much of the city was levelled during the Blitz of November 1940. Southampton was a prime target because of its general strategic importance as a major port and industrial area, and particularly because the Supermarine Spitfire was designed, developed and built in Southampton; 476 tons of bombs were dropped on the city by the Luftwaffe. The Spitfire factory was destroyed, killing many people. One building that survived the bombing was Southampton's oldest, St Michaels Church. The spire was an important navigational aid for the German pilots and consequently they were ordered to avoid hitting it.

In July 1943, a military exercise called Harlequin tested the port's ability to embark troops and equipment. Previous estimates were that 11,000 troops could be embarked on each high tide; the exercise showed that as many as 44,000 troops could in fact be handled. By D-Day, that figure had increased to 53,750 troops and 7,070 vehicles. After D-Day, Southampton continued to work at full capacity to re-supply the Allied Forces on mainland Europe.

Southampton was awarded city status in 1964, and today is still an important ocean liner port, frequented by luxury ships such as P&O's MV Oriana, and Cunard's RMS Queen Mary 2, MS Queen Victoria and MS Queen Elizabeth.

Ocean Liner ISTOCK

FAMOUS LOCALS

FACE TO FACE...

The painter **Sir John Everett Millais** was born in Southampton in 1829. Young John displayed extraordinary talent and gained himself a place at the Royal Academy aged just 11. He went on to help form the Pre-Raphaelite Brotherhood, who devoted themselves to intensity of colour and intricate detail that was considered distasteful by some. Millais became the most famous and controversial of the group with his *Christ in the House of His Parents* (1850), a realistic depiction of the Holy Family as labourers in Joseph's carpentry workshop. The painting was considered blasphemous by many critics, including Charles Dickens, who thought Millais' Mary 'ugly'. A few years later, John found himself embroiled in another scandal when Effie, the wife of art critic and

Sir John Everett Millais CREATIVE COMMONS

supporter of the Pre-Raphaelites, John Ruskin, left her husband to marry Millais. Ruskin gave him rather more cutting reviews after that! A gallery at the Southampton Institute, which opened in 1996 along with an exhibition to mark the centenary of Millais' death, bears the artist's name.

The British Labour Party politician **John Stonehouse** was born in Southampton in 1925 and educated at Taunton's College in the Upper Shirley area. His mother was the sixth female mayor of Southampton. John joined the Labour Party aged 16, went on to become Labour MP for Wednesbury in 1957, and occupied a number of different positions in government. But he is best known for attempting to fake his own death in 1974 after his business empire collapsed, leaving a pile of clothes on a Miami beach, leading to the belief that he had drowned or fallen victim to a shark attack, while in reality he had run away to Australia with his secretary. Using several false names, he transferred large sums of money between banks in further attempts to cover his tracks, but was arrested just over a month later on Christmas Eve. Stonehouse's undercover adventures didn't stop there – it was publicly revealed in 2008, 20 years after his death, that he had been a paid Czech spy since 1962.

During his childhood in Upper Shirley, John may well have rubbed shoulders with one of British comedy's best-loved figures, **Benny Hill**, who was born there in 1924 and also attended Taunton's College. Going to watch local comics with his father at the city's theatres, and seeing the abundance of pretty girls clapping and laughing, he decided to become a professional funnyman. Over the glorious career that followed, he created a host of timeless characters, 'made the whole world laugh', and inspired actors and comedians for generations to come.

Benny Hill SHUTTERSTOCK

Benny lived out his last years in his mother's house in Westrow Road until his death on 18 April 1992, and is buried at Hollybrook Cemetery, close to his birthplace. Plans for a commemorative statue in his hometown have been in the pipeline for several decades, and although nothing has been confirmed, rumour has it that sculptor **Graham Ibbeson** has lovingly fashioned a 6ft 6in Benny as his famous commissionaire Fred Scuttle, but it has yet to find a home.

Ken Russell, born in Southampton in 1927, was a film and television director renowned for his edgy and flamboyant style. He dabbled in dance and photography before his amateur films got him noticed by the BBC, where he made arts documentaries and films based on the lives of famous composers and painters, or works of art, including an Oscar-winning adaptation of D.H. Lawrence's *Women in Love* (1969). His feature films were often criticised for mixing themes of sexuality and religion.

However, Ken was not one to take it lying down. When licentious scenes in *The Devils* (1971) led critic Alexander Walker to describe the film as 'monstrously indecent' in a live TV interview, he received a whack over the head with a rolled-up copy of the Evening Standard, the paper for which he wrote, from the disgruntled

Women-in-love

director. Ken became a visiting fellow at the University of Southampton in 2007, where he advised graduate film students on their projects. He died in November 2011.

Another luminary of film, **Suzie Templeton**, was born in Hampshire in 1967 and raised in Highfield, Southampton. As a child, she enjoyed creating special effects for home movies with her brother, but it was not until Suzie's mother introduced her to stop-motion animation heroes Wallace and Gromit did she develop a passion for animation, and began working with her own models. While studying at the Royal College of Art, she created her first two short films, *Stanley* (1999) and *Dog* (2001). However, she is best known for writing and directing a modern interpretation of Sergei Prokofiev's *Peter and the Wolf* (2006), working with over 100 animators and artists to reintroduce the classic children's story to a new generation using puppets, polystyrene landscapes, and a forest made of real baby trees. It was shown at cinemas with a live orchestra performing the original score from 1936, and won the Academy Award for Best Short Film in 2008, amongst others.

Though few have heard of erstwhile Southampton local **Charles William Miller**, without him Brazil may not have become the football-loving nation it is today. Charles was born in Brazil in 1874 to a Scottish father and an English mother. Children of British expatriates were commonly sent 'home' for their schooling, so Charles left the little town of São Paulo for Southampton in 1884, aged nine, to attend the Banister Court public school. There, he discovered football and became a dedicated and skilful player, playing for and against the great amateur team the Corinthians and also St Mary's, known today as Southampton FC. Charles returned to Brazil 10 years later, carrying with him two footballs and a copy of the Hampshire FC rules – only to find that nobody knew how to play. All it took was an afternoon with a group of friends divided into two teams, a quick run-down of the rules, for the whole town – and within a few years, all of Brazil – to go football mad.

Bibliography

BALDOCK, DOROTHY, *A Taste of Hampshire and Wiltshire*, 1995, J. Salmon

Collected Memories of Hampshire: Personal Memories inspired by the Francis Frith Collection, 2013, The Francis Frith Collection

The Complete Atlas of the British Isles, 1965, The Reader's Digest Association

HINTON, DAVID AND DR A.N. NOBLE, *Hampshire and the Isle of Wight*, 1988, George Philip/Ordnance Survey

LEGG, PENNY, *Haunted Southampton*, 2011, The History Press

RANCE, ADRIAN, *Shire County Guide: Hampshire*,1988, Shire Publications Ltd

VAN DER KISTE, JOHN, *A Grim Almanac of Hampshire*, 2011, The History Press

WILSON, SIR JAMES, KCSI,*The Dialect of the New Forest in Hampshire*, 1913, Oxford University Press

WINN, CHRISTOPHER, *I Never Knew That About England,* 2005, Random House

WOOD, ROBERT, *Walks into History*, 2009, Countryside Books

http://www.britannica.com/EBchecked/topic/556463/Southampton (accessed 6/8/14)
http://www.saintsfc.co.uk/club/history/ (accessed 5/8/14)
http://www.virtualtourist.com/travel/Europe/United_Kingdom/England/Hampshire/Southampton-305277/Things_To_Do-Southampton-TG-C-3.html (accessed 8/8/14)
http://www.seacitymuseum.co.uk/wp-content/uploads/Titanic-Trail-MAY.pdf (accessed 2/8/14)
http://www.plimsoll.org/ (last accessed 8/8/14)
http://en.wikipedia.org/wiki/R._J._Mitchell (accessed 7/8/14)
http://www.discoversouthampton.co.uk/uploads/media_items/old-town-walk.original.pdf (accessed 29/6/14)
www.visit-southampton.co.uk (accessed 1/6/14)
http://en.wikipedia.org/wiki/Benny_Hill (accessed 22/7/14)
http://www.ageasbowl.com/cricket/ (accessed 22/7/14)
http://www.southamptonmaritimefestival.com/ (accessed 7/8/14)
http://www.southamptonboatshow.com/2013/home.aspx (accessed 2/8/14)
http://www.discoversouthampton.co.uk/visit/whats-on/2014/08/02/aberdeen-asset-management-cowes-week (accessed 28/7/14)
http://en.wikipedia.org/wiki/History_of_Southampton (accessed 3/8/14)